THis Book Belong's to Lakiyesha

THis Book Belong's to Lakiyesha

CORETTA SCOTT

Poetry by

NTOZAKE SHANGE

Paintings by

KADIR NELSON

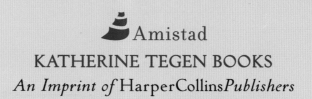

Amistad

KATHERINE TEGEN BOOKS

An Imprint of HarperCollinsPublishers

The illustrations for this book were painted with oil paints on birch plywood.

Coretta Scott

Text copyright © 2009 by Ntozake Shange

Illustrations copyright © 2009 by Kadir Nelson

Printed in the United States of America.

Library of Congress Cataloging-in-Publication Data

Shange, Ntozake.

Coretta Scott / by Ntozake Shange ; illustrated by Kadir Nelson.—1st ed.

p.   cm.

ISBN 978-0-06-125364-5 (trade bdg.) — ISBN 978-0-06-125365-2 (lib. bdg.)

1. King, Coretta Scott, 1927–2006—Juvenile literature. 2. African American women civil rights workers—Biography—Juvenile literature.

3. Civil rights workers—United States—Biography—Juvenile literature. 4. African Americans—Biography—Juvenile literature. 5. King, Martin

Luther, Jr., 1929–1968—Juvenile literature. 6. African Americans—Civil rights—History—20th century—Juvenile literature. 7. Civil rights

movements—United States—History—20th century—Juvenile literature. I. Nelson, Kadir, ill. II. Title.

E185.97.K47S53 2009   2008010486

[B]—dc22   CIP

                                                                                                                                                      AC

Typography by Martha Rago

1   2   3   4   5   6   7   8   9   10

First Edition

To my mama, Eloise, my father, P. T.,

and my daughter, Savannah

——N.S.

For my wife, Keara

Love, Kadir

some southern mornings

the moon

sits like an orange

sliver by the treetops

Coretta and her siblings
walked all
of five miles to
the nearest colored school
in the darkness
with the dew dampening
their feet

white school bus
left a
funnel of dust
on their faces
but
songs and birds of all colors

and rich soil
where slaves sought freedom
steadied them
in the face of danger

over years

learning and freedom

took hold of Coretta's soul

till she knew in her being

that the Good Lord intended freedom

for the Negro

Martin Luther King Jr. a young preacher
prayed for freedom
Coretta prayed
two minds attracted in prayer
yes they could do something
among the many
who thought moral power
would overturn Jim Crow
they prayed together
found joy
and were married

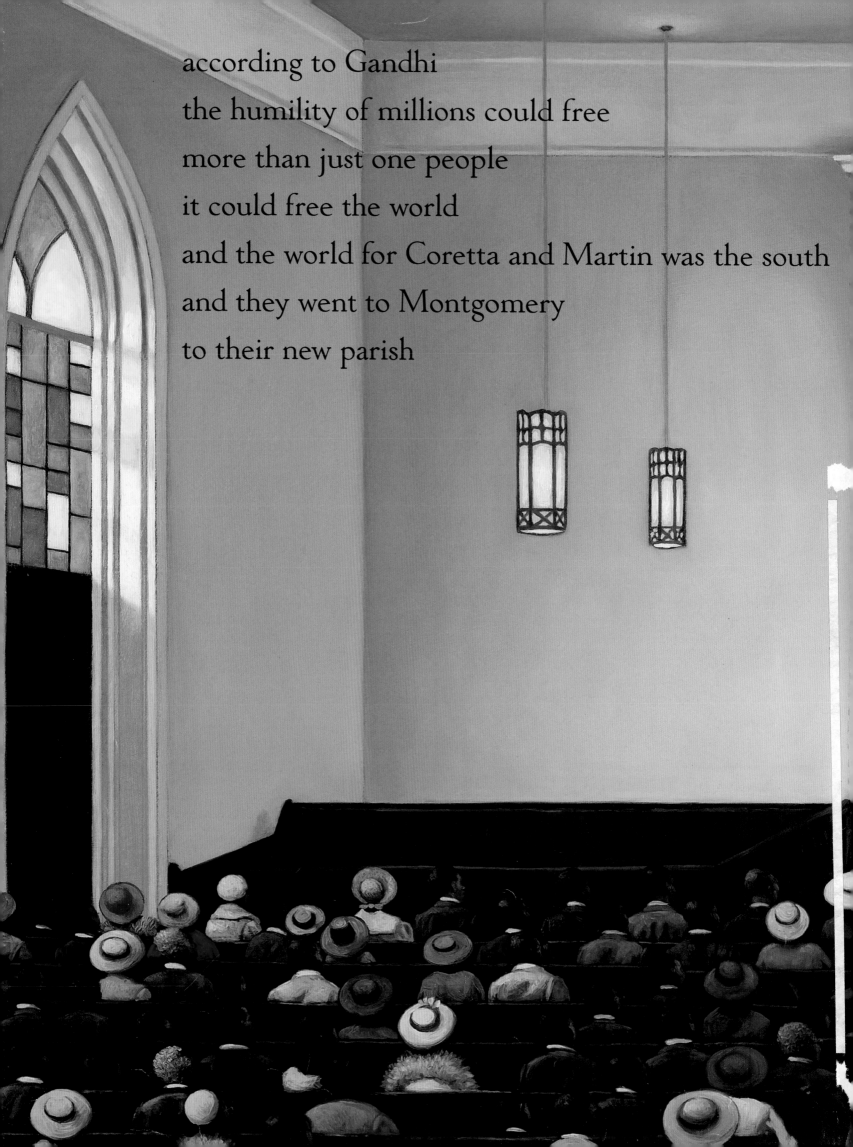

according to Gandhi

the humility of millions could free

more than just one people

it could free the world

and the world for Coretta and Martin was the south

and they went to Montgomery

to their new parish

and the Montgomery bus boycott
just the beginning
of a long journey

more boycotts and sit-ins
for many many Negro students
felt bound to do something
there were hundreds and thousands
left behind

Negroes in shacks
and cotton fields
living in fear for their lives
while they dreamed about the north

hundreds then thousands
white and black
marched
in Alabama

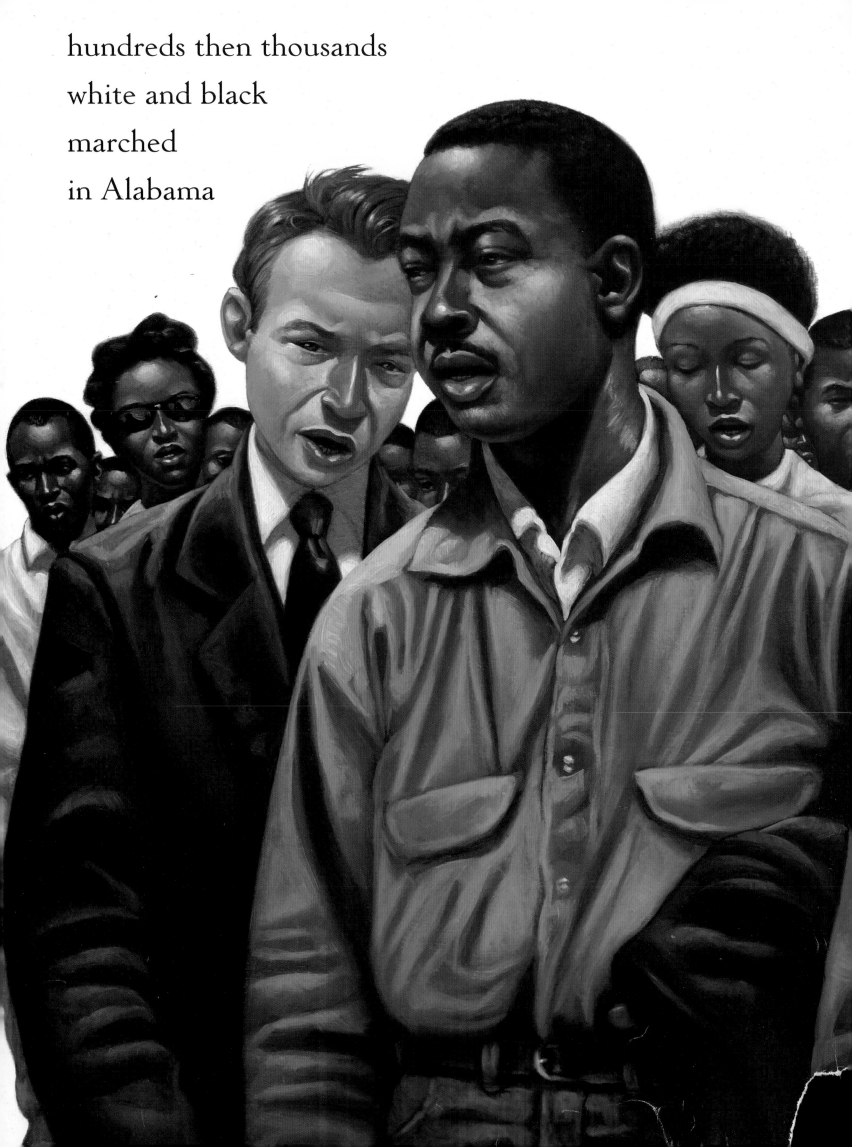

Carolina
Georgia
and Chicago

a quarter of a million at the March on Washington
peacefully singing "we shall overcome"
and listening to the words
that would inspire a nation

but fervor for the coming vote
and equality
pushed Coretta to a peace and wonderment
of the Lord
"ain't gonna let nobody turn me round
turn me round"

things nature never intended

a child to see

haunted them

tragedy accompanies growth

no matter who we are

and the Negroes are no different

"ain't gonna let nobody turn me round
gonna keep on a-walkin'
keep on a-talkin'
walkin' up to freedom land"

singin' always singin'

CORETTA SCOTT KING was born in Alabama on April 27, 1927. As a child, Coretta and her brother and sister walked five miles to the nearest school for Negroes, the term used at the time for black people. The bus carrying white children passed them each morning on the way to the white school. This division of the races is called segregation, and many states enforced segregation through Jim Crow laws.

Growing up in a family of deep faith, Coretta often sang in church, her beautiful voice soaring. At Antioch College, Coretta became interested in the idea of civil rights, or the fair treatment of all people, black and white, as American citizens. She later went on to Boston University to study concert singing. In Boston, Coretta met a theology student, Martin Luther King, Jr., who was also interested in civil rights. They were soon married. Martin introduced Coretta to the writings of Mahatma Gandhi, who believed that nonviolence was the true path to liberation for an oppressed people.

One afternoon in Montgomery, Alabama, a black seamstress, Rosa Parks, refused to give up her seat on the bus to a white man. Rosa Parks was arrested, and the South was never the same. Martin organized the Montgomery bus boycott and awakened the whole nation to the injustices of segregation.

Coretta and Martin were committed to nonviolent resistance. The hallmark of their teamwork was the March on Washington in 1963. They wanted to show the world that America was not the place it claimed to be—that everyone was not in fact "free."

Together, Coretta and Martin raised a family and worked tirelessly to further their vision. Coretta used her musical talents in a series of acclaimed Freedom Concerts that told the story of civil rights in the United States and also raised funds for the movement. In 1964 and 1965, Congress voted to approve laws that would make segregation illegal and enable blacks to vote.

On April 4, 1968, Martin went to Memphis, Tennessee, to support striking sanitation workers. Martin was on his motel balcony when a shot rang out. News of his assassination hit the streets, and cities all over the country went up in flames. Coretta was steadfast despite the violence. She left their four children in Atlanta and led the sanitation workers in a march. Until her death on January 30, 2006, Coretta spent her days speaking out for racial and economic justice and helping to build The King Center, a living memorial that provides programs to educate people about the philosophies of nonviolence. Her courage and vision are an inspiration to all.

—Ntozake Shange